Thomas Oliver Thompson

Food Frauds

Simple Methods of Detecting Adulterations in What we Consume

Thomas Oliver Thompson

Food Frauds
Simple Methods of Detecting Adulterations in What we Consume

ISBN/EAN: 9783744646420

Printed in Europe, USA, Canada, Australia, Japan

Cover: Foto ©Andreas Hilbeck / pixelio.de

More available books at **www.hansebooks.com**

FOOD FRAUDS.

SIMPLE METHODS OF DETECTING ADULTERA-
TIONS IN WHAT WE CONSUME.

"Adulteration is a wide-spread evil, which has invaded every branch of
commerce; everything which can be mixed or adulterated or debased in
any way is debased."—DR. NORMANDY.

COMPILED BY THOS. O. THOMPSON.

PRICE 25 CENTS.

CHICAGO, ILL.
RUSSELL & THOMPSON, 182 AND 184 DEARBORN ST.
1 8 8 2 .

INTRODUCTORY.

Our object in publishing this work is two-fold. First, to benefit mankind, and, second, to make money. Allowing five persons to each family, there are 10,000,000 families in the United States, according to the last census: and if the head of each buys a copy of this work, our object will most assuredly have been fully accomplished.

It would be difficult, to compute in how many of these domestic circles there are sufferings arising from the consumption of adulterated food, but if the number were known, the figures would be startling. Dyspepsia and other disorders of the stomach may be found in almost every family, and people are being gradually poisoned by adulterations of a very dangerous character. The worst feature of the case is that people have only a very slight idea of the extent to which their health is being impaired by food frauds. Bodily disorders are almost invariably attributed to other than the right causes. If the truth were known, the derangements are due and traceable to the poisonous stuffs that are mixed with the food we eat and the liquids we consume.

Pure articles are produced, but they are like two grains of wheat in a bushel of chaff—few and limited in comparison with the multitudinous trash thrown upon the market.

This work is issued with a view of calling attention to these adulterations and placing within the knowledge of everybody simple, unscientific methods of determining whether tne articles used in every household are pure as represented by a seller. It is designed to arouse the attention of the public to the enormity of the practice of adulterations, and enabling the learned, as well as the unlearned, to ascertain at any time when they are not only being swindled, but swallowing articles that are subtle and sure in their poisonous character. The question is not only merely of health, but also of commercial integrity. The purchaser should have what he calls for. If he pays for coffee, for instance, he should receive pure coffee for his money, and not an article in which some foreign substance is almost the leading ingredient.

In the presentation of the facts and methods of ascertaining adulterations we claim no originality. Most of the work is simply a compilation of facts from the most authentic and reliable sources and its presentation in a condensed and convenient form. The tests given are easy and simple, and hereafter people need not be blindly mislead in their purchases.

To know a swindle is to avoid it. To avoid a swindle is to annihilate it, and to annihilate a swindle in the form of food adulterations is to annihilate disease and premature death.

THOMAS O. THOMPSON.

CHICAGO, Ill,, January, 1882.

SUGAR.

Sugar is an article found in every household. So extensive is its use that it may be said to be one of prime necessity and wisely considered out of the category of luxuries as tea and coffee. It is estimated by that distinguished economist. David A. Wells, that the present (1881) annual production of the world is 5,500,000 tons. Of this amount, the United States and Great Britain together consume one-third. The United States produce a large quantity, but still it is obliged to import every year large amounts, the extent of which may be judged from the statement that the value of our sugar importations in 1880 was $79,153,000. Great Britain produces no sugar, and in 1878 her importations amounted to $101,234,000. Where so large quantities are consumed, the temptations for adulterations and excessive profits are strong, and importers as well as dealers seem to vie with each other in foisting upon the market a spurious article. The competition in this line has been so strong that the producers and shippers in foreign climes have resorted to tricks in order to take advantage of the market and imposed upon our government in running into this market sugars falsely colored to evade the high tariff rates. In the inspection of sugar, color is the legal test, and yet in Cuba and Demarara methods have been devised for so coloring the high grade sugars as to practically get them here under a very small duty.

The adulterations that are most commonly known are with glucose, starch, sand, chalk or whiting, bone-dust, potato sugar, gum, dextrin, finely-powdered marble and common salt. These various articles are quite cheap, and used more or less extensively according to the greed of the seller. Weight is a great desideratum where fraud is practiced, and so the heaviest material is most generally used with the mixture. If large-grained sugars were produced altogether, the perpetration of fraud would be exceedingly difficult. The detection could then be easily made by the consumer, but the small-grained sugars are mostly produced, and they mix easily with the glucose and other spurious substances. "A large-grained sugar on the other hand is a most refractory material for these little manipulations; its crystals, no matter how mingled with contaminating agents, never ceasing to manifest their native brilliancy, and thus proclaiming the fraud. It is the most easy, then, to understand why the grocer, as a rule, does not encourage these large-grained sugars. He cannot 'handle' them, and therefore brands them with fault. He says they are deficient in saccharine matter—that they will not sweeten."

'Handling' consists not only in mixing with sugar the foreign bodies already named, but in mixing together in various proportions, "sugar of different qualities and prices- as moist sugars with dry ones, very brown sugars with those of light color—the resulting article presenting a tolerable appearance to the eye, but being rarely what it professes to be—real Jamaica or Demerara sugar."

Raw sugar should never be used. Its impurities consist of live animalculæ, sporules of fungus, grit, woody fiber, etc., and hence the brown sugars of commerce are in a state wholly unfit for consumption—organic and inorganic filth abounding in them. In some samples, there have been found no less than 40,000 living insects per pound!

The chemist of the city of Chicago, Dr. Paton, recently examined thirty samples of various brands of cane sugar and found in some of them starch sugar, which he declares decidedly objectionable owing to its purgative action, gum, dextrin, marble, sand, and traces of salt; but in a number of the specimens not such an amount of impurities as to render the use of the sugars very dangerous. He declares, however, that he has "distinct objection against the use of brown sugars." In one sample he found a trace of poisonous copper, but its presence he attributed to the pan in which it was manufactured. As to brown sugar of the inferior sort all chemists agree. They would banish them from the market These sugars contain substances that are not only disgusting to the feelings of those who know their ingredients, but very injurious to the health when consumed. Cheap grades of purified sugar are being yearly more extensively introduced, and as soon as people are more generally posted the lower sorts will largely pass out of the market. Sugar insects, which abound so largely in all these lower forms of saccharine matter, should be banished from the larder of every household that values health.

Tests.—To determine the impurities in sugar is a simple one. Of course the component parts can only be detected by chemical processes. If foreign substances be present, dissolve the sugar in water. All the substances named, except gum and salt, are insoluble; and hence, after allowing a sufficient length of time for the sugar to thoroughly dissolve, the foreign articles will subside to the bottom, and can be easily detected with the eye. If there are no sediments, it can be taken for granted that there has been no special "handling" of the sugar. If it be desired to know if gum be present, proceed as follows: "Five grammes of the sugar must be dissolved in boiling spirits of wine. The greater part of the gum will remain undissolved and may be identified by its general character of stickiness."

TEA.

Tea has properly been classed among the luxuries. It is in no sense a necessity, except at ladies' gatherings, or as habit may have made its use second nature, as a pleasant and harmless stimulant. Only the best qualities are to be found on the tables of the rich and prosperous. The humble dwellings of the poor rarely contain it, unless it be the lower and almost valuless grades.

It is an article foreign to our soil, and once ranked among the dutiable articles of commerce. The duty imposed practically inhibited the use of it among the poorer classes. If they ever sipped of the tea infusion, they drank simply a decoction of exhausted tea leaves or foreign leaves mixed with "lie-tea."

Some years ago, a cargo of tea was recovered from the ocean, after it had lain for a long period, and after being duly "doctored" by experts it was placed upon the market in Chicago. Its value was almost nil, but it was sold at a low but still a very profitable figure, and taken almost entirely by poor people. One lot was sold to a contractor, and he in turn proceeded to sell it to the county at the rate of $1.25 per pound!

Genuine, finely flavored tea is too expensive for general consumption. Even then, where the "best" quality is secured, there is no assurance that it is the best tea produced. A story is told at Washington that the Chinese minister, with his interpeter, called at the house of the Secretary of State, when the latter's daughter offered him a cup of tea. The minister drank the tea and remarked very coolly: "It is of medium quality; I will send you some that is really fine." The next day she received, with his compliments, two pretty boxes of tea and a pair of vases of exquisitely carved white wood. The diplomat afterward explained that only the Chinese grandees get the best quality of tea. Foreigners may pay what they choose, but they cannot get anything above second grade.

Of this fact no stronger proof need be given than that of the total value of tea importations in 1880, which amounted to $18,917,705, a very large portion was from the average crop. Hence the desire of dealers not only to produce a spurious article for the lower as well as the upper classes, but so produce the mixture as to realize handsome profits. Their wants, to a certain extent, are met by the ingenious devices of the Chinese and Japanese. They ship various kinds, as may be desired, but what they have failed to adulterate, the dealers here "doctor," to meet requirements in business. They know that only connosseurs can detect the fraud, and between tricksters in the Orient and sharpers in the Occident, the general consumer of tea falls an easy victim. The experiment of Le Duc, in South Carolina, was in the direction of cheapening eventually the plant to the people, and supplying a pure article, but, after a large and reckless expense to the government, he succeeded in fully demonstrating that tea cannot be successfully raised in America.

The teas known to commerce are black and green. The former is grown upon the slopes of hills and ledges of mountains, while the latter is raised in manured soils. The different varieties are produced by processes in the preparation and roasting of the leaves and by methods of mixing pure leaves with foreign leaves. The principal kinds of pure black tea are Pekoe, which is the best quality, consisting of the unexpanded leaves and buds, Congou, Souchong, Caper and Bohea, the commonest description. The chief varieties of green tea are Twankay, Hyson, Young Hyson, Hyson Skin, Imperial and Gunpowder, which last corresponds in black tea with Flowery Pekoe.

The adulterations of these teas are made with—

Foreign leaves, as those of ash, plum, sloe, beech, box, elm, horse chestnut, plane, bastard plane, fancy oak, willow, poplar, hawthorn and sycamore.

Lie-tea, which consists in part of dust of tea leaves in

some cases, but more frequently foreign leaves, sand, quartz
and magnetic oxide of iron, being made by means of a solution of starch into little sizes in imitation of different kinds
of tea.

Mineral substances, chiefly sand, quartz, turmeric, magnetic oxide of iron, while china clay, soapstone, Prussian
blue, chromate of lead, carbonate of copper, sulphate of
iron to increase the astringency, and other mineral matter
are employed in artificial coloration or painting of teas
both black and green.

A traveler through China says: "The Chinese in the
neighborhood of Canton are able to prepare a tea which can
be colored and made up to imitate various qualities of green
tea;" and this and similar practices prevail not only in
China but also in this country. Green tea is extensively
manufactured from damaged black leaves. Twankay tea is
often mixed with false leaves, which are colored with indigo,
and calcined foliated gypsum. Instances are known where
persons have been employed to secure exhausted leaves of
the genuine at hotels, restaurants, boarding houses and other
places, and these leaves so obtained have been thoroughly
rinsed with a solution of gum and re-dried. After drying the
leaves were mixed—if for black tea, with rose pink and
black lead to face them. Of eighteen samples secured from
tea dealers in Chicago, the city chemist found that ash pre-
dominated in all, and there was noticeable the presence of
foreign, exhausted or re-dried tea leaves and mineral matters used for coloring.

TESTS.—Chemical analysis only can best determine the
kinds of substances used in the adulterations. A simple
test, however, which will easily disclose the purity of the
tea, according to Dr. Hassall, of England, is to boil the tea
for some time, and then closely examine the leaves. If
foreign leaves be present, they easily separate and show by
their general nature their difference from the genuine. A
comparison with a true leaf will always reveal the foreign
one. If the leaves are exhausted ones, one can determine it
with the eye, by the fact that the fold or roll of leaves is less

regular and uniform than that of the unused tea, and many flat pieces of leaves occur, the surfaces being often aggluti-nated together.

Lie-tea will reveal itself by pouring upon the masses a lit-tle boiling water, when, if they consist of leaves, they will quickly unfold and expand, whereas, if of lie-tea, they will break down and become disintegrated, leaving a dirty resi-due in which minute particles of the tea-leaf are visible. If it be mixed with quartz or sand and magnetic oxide of iron, place one of the little masses between the teeth and it will feel gritty, and if the finger be pressed upon them when ren-dered soft by the action of hot water, the sand or other min-eral matter will be at once felt. If iron be present, spread the powder on paper and a magnet drawn across it will bring the particles to the edge of the paper; or plunge the magnet into the powdered tea and it will bring up the min-eral particles.

To determine if the tea has been faced, a portion of it may be washed with cold water, the washings being set aside for a time, when the substances removed from the surface of the leaves will gradually subside to the bottom of the glass.

If Prussian blue has been used for coloring, it may be recognized under the microscope by the angular form of the fragments, their brilliant and transparent blue color. If turmeric has been used, it will be noticed under the micro-scope, as of characteristic yellow cells, of a rounded form, which are filled with starch granules of a peculiar shape. If black lead is present, the jet black, glossy and metallic lus-tre imparted to the tea coated with it will serve in most cases for identification. To determine precisely, remove a thin slice from the surface of one of the leaves and place it under the microscope; if there is black lead, the sample will appear thickly studded with numerous black particles.

COFFEE.

A cup of coffee is an almost indispensable adjunct at every breakfast table. As Lord Beaconsfield has said: "A cup of good coffee is the rarest and most delicious beverage in the world." At whatever sacrifice of other luxuries, the humblest and poorest person demands his coffee to round off and give tone to his simple repast. Since it enters so generally and extensively into the requirements of a family, there is every reason why it should be of at least a good quality, but the very fact of its being in general demand has lead to very extensive and wholesale adulterations. The importations during 1880 were valued at $56,777,625, and once in the hands of some of our unscrupulous dealers, a large portion of the coffee has been subjected to legerdemain, which other substances so nearly allied in taste has rendered easy. Where the seeds or berries are purchased by the consumer and closely examined, the chances for fraud are nearly out of question, except where an inferior grade is mixed with a still lower grade. Arabian or Mocha coffee are distinguished by their yellow color and comparative smallness and roundness. Martinique are larger than Arabian seeds, rounded on the ends, of greenish color, and retain the thin skin, which comes off by roasting. The seeds of San Domingo coffee have their two extremities pointed. Those of Java or East Indian coffee are larger and of a paler yellow, while those of Ceylon, West Indian and Brazilian coffee possess a blueish or greenish grey tint.

Of course the mixing together of the lower and higher grades produces an inferior article, but it is in the ground or powdered product where adulteration is most practiced. The most common practice of adulteration is with cheap chicory. In most cases it forms the largest proportion of the mixture, and is easily disguised with coffee. Its flavor is imperceptible and the fraud readily passes for the genuine. Some dealers, with an air of innocence, grind the coffee in the presence of purchasers, but such a procedure is no guarantee that the product is genuine, as they manage to adroitly slip into it such quantities of chicory as they deem expedient. Some have chicory apartments in their coffee mills, and while the genuine berry is ostensibly being reduced to a powder the chicory is also being ground with it. Even though there are no secret apartments and the berries themselves are examined, the purchaser is liable to be deceived, as it has been stated that a patent has been taken out to mould chicory into the form of coffee berries.

Sometimes rye, roasted peas, wheat, corn and beans and roasted carrots, parsnips and mangold wurzel are ground and mixed with coffee. Occasionally acorns, sawdust, oak bark tan, croats and baked liver are used. In order to give color and taste to the adulterations, burnt sugar, lampblack and venetian red are employed.

TESTS.—It is an easy matter to ascertain whether the suspected article is adulterated. If the ground coffee, says Dr. Hassall, cakes in the paper in which it is folded, or when pressed between the fingers, there is good reason to believe that it is adulterated, most likely with chicory. If a few pinches of the suspected coffee are placed upon some water in a wine glass, the coffee floats on the surface and the other substances gradually fall to the bottom to a greater or less extent. The coffee does not rapidly imbibe the water, while the other particles being more porous absorb it. If the cold water, to which a portion of ground coffee has been added quickly, becomes deeply colored, it is an evidence of the presence of some roasted vegetable substance or burnt sugar, for when coffee is only added to water, it becomes scarcely colored for some time. Not only does the solution become dark colored, but if a boiling water solution be made, it will be thick and mucilaginous if it be adulterated with any substance containing much gum and starch, but the infusion of coffee will be found thin and limpid. Chicory has more than three times the coloring power of highly-roasted coffee; maize double that of coffee, while peas and beans have only half the coloring power.

Again, spread a few grains on a piece of glass with a few drops of water, and if you can pick out with a needle small soft pieces, the coffee is adulterated. When by any of these processes the results follow as stated, there is no doubt of adulterations. The character of the adulterations can only be determined by the microscope.

HONEY.

The production and accumulation of honey is a slow process, but the encouragement given to it in the market in the past has lead to the establishment of apiaries on all well-regulated farms and elsewhere. The supply has always been about equal to the demand. In view of such a state of affairs, and the further fact that it leads all sweets, it would be supposed that no attempts at adulteration would be made, and that the cunning devices of men would be baffled. Not so. Shrewd chemists and speculators have been equal to the emergency. They have overcome all difficulties, and placed upon the market a spurious article that defies detection with the general purchaser. In fact it has been stated that even the comb has been so well made by means of delicate machinery that when it is filled with the manufactued honey, it has all the appearance of the genuine, and that manufactories are now in existence for the artificial manufacture of the entire product. As to the truth of this, some doubts exist in the minds of honey producers, but as to the honey part, it is a well known fact that its manufacture has grown into very large proportions. Glucose is the leading ingredient; in some cases almost the sole ingredient. Prof. A. J. Cook, of the Michigan Agricultural College, says: ''It is said that all our sugars, with the exception of the granulated, are largely composed of this artificial glucose. Reputable authority asserts the same to be true of nearly all our table syrups; and much of the so-called honey on the markets is largely composed of this same grape sugar. Yet no sign of these wicked frauds is to be seen on the labels. If not pronounced pure, the purchaser is left to infer that such is the case. This state of things is a disgrace to our civilization, and should be denounced as base and corrupting by every honest man. Laws, State and National, should be enacted and enforced, so that all who practice these adulterations and thus sell articles under a false trade mark, should receive condign punishment.''

This adulteration is not for the purpose of bettering the condition of honey, but simply with a view of bringing the dealers large profits. It is claimed that glucose is mixed with honey, because it contains the same chemical properties as honey, and insures its durability, but experts hold that such is not the case, for the reason that, if glucose has any merits of its own, it would stand alone and compete with other sweets, and not be used solely for adulterating purposes. How largely glucose has come to be used as an adulterating article may be judged from the statement that the industry has grown from 100 bushels of corn daily to the present use of 6,000 bushels per day. The annual production in 1881 was 600,000,000 pounds, and the amount of money invested in the business is said to be about $20,-000,000.

A building for its manufacture has now been nearly completed in this city, which stands the highest in point of stories, and almost the lagest in Chicago. When in operation it will daily turn out thousands of pounds. A great deal of the glucose produced in the United States has been sold to dealers in honey, as well as in sugars and syrups, and the rest has found its way to breweries and distilleries, to be used as substitutes for more expensive articles, and to candy makers, fruit preservers, druggists and patent medicine dealers.

TESTS.—Prof. Cook gives the following as a test of the adulteration of honey: ''It is a well known fact that most kinds of honey will granulate or crystalize whenever the temperature is reduced below freezing, or even a higher degree than 32 deg. Fahrenheit. A few kinds of honey, like that from the famous white sage of California, will not granulate, but this is so exceptional that the candying test, as so often urged by M. Dadant, is a pretty sure one, and is by far the most practical one that has been suggested. Honey, that as winter approaches, becomes solid, may be considered as pure. If it remains fluid it may well be regarded as suspicious. It is stated that the Thurbers first used glucose to preserve the fluid condition of the honey, as granulated honey was objected to by their customers. Of course they were not slow to appreciate the further gain of selling glucose at double its market value. Mr. Dadant, then, is right in urging people to purchase only granulated honey, unless they purchase comb. Extracted honey, if granulated, may be reliquified by setting the vessel containing it into hot water, that is not more than 180 deg. Fahrenheit for an hour or more. Caution is required that the vessel containing the honey shall be entirely surrounded by water, so that the honey shall not be overheated at the bottom of the vessel. In this way candied honey can be reliquified with no loss of flavor or quality. If after reducing it, it is kept in a warm place, it will not solidify again.

As already stated, the adulteration is done by the dealers. Once started, as suggested above, the excessive gains to the wholesale dealer secured its continuance until the sharp detectives over the sea brought the iniquitous practice to light. Yet the evil is by no means abated by the dealers. Hence another way to detect the pure from the spurious. If honey is offered for sale in a neat glass jar, with the trade mark of a New York or Chicago dealer, it may well be tested, especially if it shows no tendency to granulate upon exposure to the cold. On the other hand, if in tin pails or common fruit cans or jelly cups, with the name of the producer on the vessel, it may be regarded safely as honey. This will readily granulate, and very likely will be solid when purchased. This should be considered as a recommendation and not as an objection."

MILK.

The sale of milk has grown into an immense industry. In the case of people living within a radius of forty or sixty miles of Chicago, or of any large city, the shipments they make realize them a considerable portion of the income upon which they depend for their support. Chicago consumes millions of gallons of milk annually, and the supply comes mainly from the country. Within the city there is a considerable production of milk, but as the cows are fed in filthy barns, in a majority of cases, upon distillery swills, only the poorer classes buy it.

The best quality and largest quantity, however, comes from verdant pastures, and the ease with which it can be adulterated is too strong a temptation not only to the grangers themselves but also to the city vendors. The close relation between milk and the "town pump" has frequently evoked criticism, and sometimes to such a degree has the lacteal fluid been diluted that it has been a question whether water or milk preponderated. But it is not the only adulteration to which milk is liable. Where a large quantity of water has been used it is often necessary to have recourse to other adulterating ingredients, as for instance, sugar to sweeten it, salt to bring out the flavor and annatto to color it.

Milk is also sometimes adulterated with chalk, starch, cerebral matter, such as calves' brains, etc., whipped into it, gum, dextrin and a decoction of boiled white carrots.

TESTS.—On the detection of water, two methods may be employed: As milk is much heavier than water, the specific gravity of the mixed or impure article is consequently much less than that of the genuine article. Place, therefore, the pure and the watered or mixed article side by side, and then float a cork with a thick wire or a darning needle through its center, in each sample. In the pure liquid the cork will not sink as deep as in the adulterated article.

Again, dip a darning or knitting needle or some polished rounded steel into the suspected article, and if it be pure, the milk will adhere evenly on all sides on being withdrawn. The microscope will reveal the kinds of substances used, as pure milk is homogeneous and contains myriads of beautifully formed globules of fatty matter of various size, reflecting the light strongly and readily soluble in caustic potash. The globules are coated with an envelope formed of some albuminous substance, and any particles foreign to milk can be easily distinguished from them. "Swill milk" can be discovered by the pale blue color it presents on standing for some time.

BUTTER.

In no article of commerce is fraud practiced in so unblushing a manner as in the sale of butter. Adulteration of butter has been practiced from time immemorial, but it is only within recent years that factories have been established for the exclusive purpose of manufacturing the spurious article. These factories have been established in the vicinity of the Stock Yards of Chicago, where the adulterating material required can be the more readily and conveniently obtained, and in the very heart of the city, where commission dealers are accessible. It would be thought that with these factories the market would be fully supplied, but so great is the greed for gain, that establishments are found in full blast in Wisconsin, Iowa and Indiana. These country manufacturers take the creamery of their neighborhoods, and, to adulterate it, have agents in the city to send them the necessary material. Chicago and its surrounding country, however, are not alone in the nefarious business. Manufactories abound all over the country. In New York City and State alone, 20,000,000 pounds of the spurious article are annually manufactured. The entire pure butter product of the State has reached in a single year, 111,018,413 pounds, and, when it is taken into account that the manufactories have a capacity for turning out 116,000,000 pounds of oleomargarine a year, it can be readily seen that the dairy business is placed in jeopardy It is also computed that there are from 5,000,000 to 8,000,000 people throughout the country interested in the dairy business, who have a capital invested in it from $4,000,000 to $6,000,000, and, as nearly every State in the union is engaged in the manufacture, the loss to these people in consequence of the competition with the spurious is enormous.

The money value of the annual dairy product is estimated by good authorities to exceed that of the wheat crop, or corn crop, and is greater than that of the cotton and wool combined and is between $400.000,000 and $600,000,000. Besides proving detrimental to home production, the adulterations injure our foreign trade. In illustration of this fact, Congressman Parker has shown by statements procured from the bureau of statistics and census bureau, that during the six years ending June 30, 1881, the value of oleomargarine exported rose from $70,483 in 1876 to $381,556 in 1881. In 1878 the quantity exported was only 1,698,401 pounds, but in the year ending June 30, 1881, it was 26,327,676 pounds. In the year ending December 31, 1881, the quantity of butter exported was only 21,331,358 pounds, while in the preceding year it was more than 37,000,000 pounds. The value of the butter exported was $3,250,000 less in 1881 than in 1880. On the other hand, the statistics show that the amount and value of cheese exported were greater in 1881 than in 1880. The inference is, of course, that the amount of butter exported has greatly decreased because of the remarkable growth of the oleomargarine industry and the rapidly increasing amount of oleomargarine exported. The census bureau furnished a statement showing that in the cities of New York, Philadelphia, Brooklyn, Chicago, Boston, Baltimore, Cincinnati, and Louisville there were twelve factories, employing nearly seven hundred hands, paying $187,648 in wages, and using $4,740,941 worth of material. The capital of these factories was $1,600,000, and the value of the annual product $6,035,753. Four-fifths of the material product of these cities are credited to New York City. Mr. Parker asserts that at home every consumer is liable to become the daily victim of those who are adulterating the people's food by an imitation so artfully made as to defy detection by any except experts, and that our market abroad for the genuine product is greatly harmed by the belief that we are palming off on consumers as a dairy product a base imitation.

The imitation butter only costs the Eastern manufacturers nine cents a pound, while it readily sells at from twenty-five to forty cents.

Apt was the cartoon in an Eastern illustrated publication,

where it represented a maid churning in a country farm-house, with the words underneath, "The Dairy of the Past," and a factory with a foreman, surrounded with boxes labeled fats, greese, lard and the refuse of packing establishments, mixing them together for butter, with the words underneath, "The Dairy of the Present."

Where so many foreign substances are used, it would seem to be an easy matter to detect the adulteration, but the coloring as well as taste are so well looked after that the fraud readily passes as butter. Lard, specially prepared, is most commonly used with pure butter, and the extent to which it enters into the composition may be judged when it is stated that in a recent trial of a dealer in Chicago, it was shown by a chemist that the sample purchased contained 70 per cent. of lard. In the trade the mixtures are known as oleomargarine, in which beef suet is the leading ingredient, used entirely uncooked; butterine, pure butter and lard; and suine, the leaf lard of the hog, which is macerated and used in its raw state, but in the market it all passes for butter. Their profits may be judged when it is stated that lard only costs in Chicago from 2½ to 17 cents per pound, while butter sells at from 18 to 50 cents per pound. In some cases, the mixtures are harmless, but in a majority of instances, the stuff is absolutely injurious from the very nature of the vile, rejected articles that constitute its ingredients. In all cases as much water as possible is incorporated in order to give weight. By bringing the butter to a melting point, water to the amount of 50 per cent. and salt from 2 to 14 per cent. are stirred into the mixture until it becomes cold. Butter is also adulterated with starch, usually potato flour, and with curd, the fat of beef, mutton, veal, etc., no matter whether from diseased or putrid carcasses, as is most frequently the case.

Inasmuch as color often determines the price, some cream-eries, where even pure butter is supposed to be prepared for the market, use a compound to give the article a rich, yellow appearance. Butter, from milk from cows off grass-feed, has a white appearance, and because of the suspicion attaching to it in that condition, color compounds are mixed with it. It is claimed by those who use them that they are prepared from vegetable substances and hence harmless, but others, who pretend to a knowledge of the matter and are opposed to the system of deception, hold that they are of an injurious nature and should not be used.

TESTS.—To determine adulteration, a sample should be taken from the center of the lump, melted and placed in a bottle. The bottle should then be placed for a half an hour or so near the fire. The water and salt will become separated from the butter and sink on account of their greater weight. As to whether there are any trustworthy chemical tests for foreign fats in butter, authorities differ. Generally the presence of lard can be detected by the whiter appearance of the mixture over pure butter, or its unnatural, peculiar coloring, and its sticky, peculiar character. An expert can determine it at once by its color and taste, good creamery having a fresher and more palatable taste. As the fusing or melting point of butter is less than that of animal fats in the ratio of about 33 to 45, the presence of fats can be very closely determined by placing the suspected article upon a hot griddle and noting the manner and rapidity with which the parts dissolve.

Furthermore, under the microscope, pure butter reveals elongated globules of fatty matter in clusters, while the spurious presents a mixed conglomerate, and greasy looking mass.

CHEESE.

The manufacture of cheese has grown enormously within the past few years. The superiority of American cheese has created a large foreign demand, and the exportations are yearly increasing on account of it. United States Commissioner Loring estimates that during the year 1881, this country shipped abroad between 120,000,000 to 140,000,000 pounds of cheese. To take advantage of this increased demand, manufacturers have resorted to extensive adulterations, and lest the reputation already achieved and the trade already acquired be destroyed, the dairy interests of the country, in local as well as national organizations, have entered their protests. They verv laudably desire the home, as well as the foreign market protected from the spurious article.

So good has been the reputation of American cheese abroad that unscrupulous dealers have taken further advantage of it, as witness the following from a recent issue of The Chicago Tribune—"The Drovers' Journal says: 'The quotations on American cheese and butter received from the Liverpool market are of no value to any one in the trade. They are utterly worthless except to convey and perpetuate a false impression. These articles are mostly in the hands of one house, and the market is as skillfully manipulated as any fancy stock in Wall Street, and by an expert who shows a smartness that would cause Jim Fisk to turn in his grave with envy. Nearly all the poor English cheese the firm handle they label American, and nearly all the prime American stock they sell is labeled prime English. Thousands of boxes of choice Illinois and Wisconsin made goods are sold annually by this firm as choice English; and the house has practiced this deception since the trade began, or since American goods made the just reputation they enjoy.'

"There is no doubt that the foreign dealer sometimes resorts to ways that are dark and tricks that are vain, but people here have set them many awful examples. The adulteration of cotton with sand, cheese and butter with lard, lard with tallow, etc., have been carried out on such a scale by unprincipled parties on this side of the Atlantic as to destroy the confidence of many in even those articles which are pure, and materially lessen the demand in not a few cases. Vast quantities of vile stuff have been sent over to Europe, and it is no wonder if the cheaters there avil themselves of the fact to their own temporary benefit. Only two days ago it was stated here by an exporter that he could not obtain orders for lard, though offering to lay it down in Liverpool at considerably less than quotations. The natural inference is that the parties corresponded with were suspicious of quality, though in that case there was no reasonable ground for fear."

The adulterations, to which resort is had, are those with lard and other animal fats, the leaves of sage, parsly and other herbs, which are so infused into the cheese as to give it a green color. Other matters, such as annatto, mangold flowers, saffron, and the juice of red carrots are likewise used for coloring. To give weight, potatoes boiled and reduced to a pulp, and bean meal are employed. The outer surface is sometimes washed over either with venetian red, and reddle or sulphate of copper and arsenic, in order to protect the cheese from the attacks of the cheese mite and other parasites. This practice is very dangerous, as many persons frequently eat the rind, and, besides, is not always a sure safeguard against parasites. The presence of parasites can be ascertained by cutting into the cheese. If dry and powdery parts be found, it can be set down that such parts consist almost entirely of cheese mites and their ova in different stages of development.

TESTS.—The differences in the composition of cheese, such as being made from cream, whole milk, or skim-milk, or made into a hard cheese or soft, like cream cheese, render it quite difficult to determine the question of purity. The presence of annatto, however, is indicated by its orange color. The use of potato and other starchy substances, as bean meal, etc., can be determined by adding to a minute portion of the cheese a drop or so of a solution of iodine. The cells of the potato are characterized by their large size and rounded form, and bean meal reveals similar characteristics. If copper has been used, burn the rind and then treat the ash with nitric acid, after which the solution may be rendered alkaline by ammonia, when a characteristic blue color will appear. The detection of arsenic can only be made by a very difficult chemical process. If fats have been used, heat the cheese in a pan of water, when the fat will separate and may be easily poured off. Venetian red can only be detected by a long chemical analysis. Pure cheese is never colored.

CONFECTIONERY.

CONFECTIONS SHARPEN AFFECTIONS.

Art and ingenuity have been taxed to produce something novel, attractive and palatable in confectionery. With pure and wholesome substances only limited varieties of candies can be manufactured, and hence we find that the dealers resort to the use of articles, which are absolutely poisonous in their character, in order to place before the public greater sorts of confections. The adulteration of sugar confectionery is enormous; and many of the ills of young people, as well as of older ones, who have a "sweet tooth," grow directly out of their consumption.

The chief varieties of articles used in adulterations are glucose, starch, lemon chrome, chalk, different kinds of clay, plaster of Paris, lampblack, chromate of lead, cochineal, red lead, red oxide of lead, vermilion, cinnabar, bisulphuret of mercury, brown ferruginous earths, Antwerp blue, indigo, ferrocyanide of iron, German ultramarine, Brunswick green, carbonate of copper, Emerald green, arsenite of copper, white lead, hydrated sulphate of lime, mixed with different kinds of flour and arrowroot. The leading adulterant is with glucose. Equal parts of sugar and glucose are used on the ground that certain kinds of candy, if made out of nothing but cane-sugar, grow hard and grow old in a very short Glucose when mixed with cane-sugar, keeps them soft and fresh. It is also claimed that it brightens up the candy.

This use of glucose now threatens a long litigation. The manufacturing confectioners have become alarmed by a claim of the National Confectionery Company of Boston for indemnity for past infringement upon what is called the Chase patent, granted in 1870, covering the use of grape-sugar in the manufacture of boiled sugar goods, and the payment of a royalty of ½ cent a pound on all glucose bought

from the Buffalo, Peoria and Glen Cove refineries, and ½ cent
a pound on all other grape-sugar purchases. The Chase
patent is believed by the manufacturers to have been sud-
denly called into action by parties controlling the Buffalo
and American grape-sugar companies in Buffalo and the
Peoria, Ill., refinery, and Duryea, of the Glen Cove works,
Long Island, to control the glucose trade of the union as
against all other manufacturers, and particularly to head off
the Chicago concern now approaching completion.   No
doubt is said to exist as to the validity of the patent and the
power of the present owners to enforce a claim for past infringement, and a future royalty from every confectioner in
the union who has been using glucose, and the impression is
that a ring has been formed to squeeze the confectioners to
buy exclusively of the companies nominally under arrange-
ments with the National Confectionery Company, and also
to extort royalty rights worth $3,000,000 a year.   The Buffalo
confectioners are joining their colleagues elsewhere and propose to raise $1,000,000, if necessary, to fight the patent.   A
wholesale confectioner has stated that on trial he will be
able to prove the use of glucose in American candies anterior
to 1867,   Such proof it is claimed will invalidate the patent.

In some samples of candies the colors are so numerous,
that in a single parcel there may be together four or five
poisons.   Nearly all the colors given are deadly poisons and
instances have been known where sickness and death have
resulted from a large use of candies colored with them.   The
essences used to flavor the candies are also of a dangerous
nature, such as pine-apple, jargonell pear or bitter almond.
The worst are prussic acid and fusel oil.   Some candies that
have a fruity taste are flavored with rotten cheese, which has
been previously treated with sulphuric acid and bichromate
of potash.

Some candies are also impregnated with intoxicating
liquors.   Recently in New Haven, Conn., it is stated that a
young lady of fine family became intoxicated by eating
candy compounded with rock and rye.   In consequence of
this discovery, the confectioner was notified by the city at-

torney, that if he continued the manufacture of the article, which was apparently solid, he must take out a liquor license. A society for the prevention of crime also interested itself in the matter and adopted measures to stop the selling of such candies.

TESTS.—The color is an indication of aduteration, but to determine whether it is vegetable, animal or mineral matter, all that is necessary is to dissolve the candy in water and whatever is precipitated to the bottom may be put down as either mineral or insoluble starch, or some insoluble substance, as chalk, white potter's clay, pipe clay or Cornish clay, etc. If plaster of Paris has been used, it becomes solid when moistened with water. Chalk will effervesce on the addition of an acid If some kind of starch has been used, dissolve a small part of the candy upon a slip of glass and if there is a residue, it can be put down as starch. If any other insoluble substance besides starch has been used, the starch can be converted into glucose with sulphuric acid.

The presence of insoluble or mineral substances is of course very objectionable.

BEER.

When Gambrinus invented this beverage, it consisted of the products of malt, hops and water. The brewing of beer, however, in these modern days, has been revolutionized, and we find such adulterations used as those with glucose, water, sugar, treacle, liquorice, burnt sugar, vegetable bitters, including picric acid, coculus indicus and strychnia; carminatives and opium, various minerals, as alum, salt, sulphate of iron, carbonate of lime, soda and other articles. Sweet flag root, quassia, coriander seeds, capsicum, caraway-seeds, grains of paradise, ginger, beans and peas, to save malt, and oyster shells are also employed. To give beer an appearance of strength, sulphate of iron alum, and salt are used ; to correct acidity, chalk and the alkalies, and to give hardness characteristic of age, sulphuric acid and cream of tartar, or bitartrate of potash.

"Beans," says a writer, "tend to mellow malt liquor, and from their properties add much to its inebriating qualities, but they must not be used in too large a quantity. Oyster shells are very good to recover sour beer. Alum is generally put into the vat, as it gives the beer a smack of age. Coculus indicus is used as a substitute for malt and hops, and is a great preservative of malt liquor. It prevents second fermentation in bottled beer and consequently the bursting of the bottles in warm climates. Its effects are of an inebriating nature." Half alum and half copperas, as well as gas, are used to give beer a head of froth.

Each brewer has a process of his own for combining the articles enumerated, and, to such an extent has adulteration been resorted to, that some of the beer sold to dealers is positively injurious. Many, who are fond of beer, are loth to drink it because of its effects, in some instances, producing billiousness and headaches, and in other cases, acting as a purgative and deranging the system. Hence the preference shown for imported beer, where it can be obtained, such as Erlanger, Culmbacher, etc. This beer produces no evil effects and must therefore be pure, or, if adulterated, composed of harmless ingredients. Some brands of home brewing are most excellent, but they are rare and not easily obtainable except at restaurants, which have built up a reputation and desire to keep it.

In New York recently, a committee of gentlemen proposed to visit several breweries of that city, and witness the process of manufacture with a view of either confirming or denying the reports in circulation, as to the poisonous character of the substances used in turning out the "amber nectar." The brewers declined on some special plea, and then a thorough chemical analysis, by some chemists, of various samples showed that the real reason for not permitting the visit was the desire to conceal the extent to which they adulterated their beer.

A leading brewer of Chicago admitted to the writer of this work the use of injurious substances, but claimed, in extenuation of his questionable practice, the fact that others did the same, and, to protect himself, and to be able to produce and sell as cheaply as others, he was forced into it much against his own will and personal inclinations. He had to do it or run his business at a pecuniary loss. The loss, however, is entirely on the side of the buyers and consumers. The adulterations are wholly for the purpose of realizing greater gains.

When it is taken into account that the value of malt liquors consumed in the United States amounted to $444,806,373 in 1881, according to the report of the bureau of statistics, it requires no stretch of the imagination to picture the immense profits resulting from the use of the foreign substances named; since the price of beer to buyers and consumers is the same as it has been for years, and the adulterating articles used are of the cheapest description. No stronger proof of the enormous practice of adulterations can be given than the almost stationary character of the cultivation of hops. In

1860, the value of malt liquors produced was only $7,994,707; in 1870, the value of the product had increased to $55,706,643 and in 1881, the value rose to over $444,000,000 as above; while the acreage of the hop crop in 1874 was 37,004, and at the present time is in the vicinity of 70,000. If hops were in as great a demand as years ago and no substitutes used in beer, it ought to follow that the acreage ought to increase in almost like proportion with the increase in the brewing of beer, especially since our exportations of hops has increased from 9,587,329 pounds in 1877, to 18,458,782 in 1878, and to nearly 26,000,000 in 1879. On the contrary, the "malt" product has grown amazingly and the acreage very slight, the former increasing since 1870 eight-fold, while the latter grew scarcely two-fold.

TESTS.—Boil the beer with some unbleached wool for about ten minutes. Remove the wool and wash it. If the beer is pure, the wool will remain white, but if it contain picric acid the wool will be dyed of a yellow color. If sulphuric acid be present, dip a pen into it and then if the written words turn black on being dried before the fire, the acid has been used. As to the use of burnt sugar, genuine beer, when shaken with a solution of tannin, becomes decolorized, while that colored with the sugar still retains a greater part of its color. If cream of tartar has been used, add to some beer, alcohol until it is not entirely dissolved on shaking, and then, after it has been allowed to stand for twenty-four hours, the crystalline residue at the bottom reveals it. The presence of coculus indicus and other substances can only be ascertained by a chemical process.

LARD.

If one could witness the manufacture of lard in some of the rendering establishments in the cities, there would be surprise and consternation. The apparently pure and white article so nicely shown in the market, would be found to be largely made of the worst animal refuse instead of from the fat only which surrounds the tissues. All substances that in any way yield fat are melted at a certain temperature, the fluid extracted running into good sized kegs. The worst feature of the manufacture is that the refuse frequently comes from hogs that have died from disease. Alum and quicklime are used to give it its white appearance, and potato flour, starch, mutton suet, tallow and carbonate of potash employed to give weight. A gentleman purchased what he considered a superior quality of lard; indeed he had never seen an article that looked better. He prepared with it an ointment, and on mixing in some chemicals, he discovered that the lard turned very shortly into a full slate color. On examination, the lard was found to contain a large portion of lime. The lard renderer subsequently stated to the party that it was a common practice among lard dealers to mix from 2 to 5 per cent. of milk of lime with the melted lard. A sopanaceous compound is formed; which is not only pearly white, but will allow a stirring in during coloring of 25 per cent. of water.

If this lard were used only in America the damage would not be so great, but a good deal of it is shipped abroad, the result is that it works great injury to this country in foreign lands. Recently Cuba, which consumes a large quantity, sent back its protest, and gave warning that unless stopped, purchases would be made elsewhere, as it did not want our adulterated grades. Of course the effect of shipping this mixed stuff has already been to diminish the foreign demand, as witness the newspaper extract in the chapter on "Cheese," and the following: In 1878, the total exports of lard amounted to 342,667,920 pounds, while in 1879 they fell off 20,955,615 pounds, although the production had greatly increased and prices ruled comparatively low.

TESTS.—To determine the lard adulteration, mix with the article some nitrate of mercury, when if it turns black it is impure.   Or, if on melting, it fuse without effervescence, or without the occurrence of a deposit, it may be safe to set it down as pure, but if ebulition takes place, or a sediment is thrown down, the lard is unquestionably adulterated.

If starch be present, mix a drop of a tincture of iodine with a few grains of the lard upon a slip of glass, when the composition will become either deep blue or almost black.

VINEGAR.

Some of the compounds sold under the name of vinegar are only such in taste. The different kinds may be designated as malt, wine, cider, beet, sugar and wood vinegars, but a large portion of the stuff offered in the market is prepared from less expensive material, and sustains no relation to the active principle from which it should derive its strength and purity. The chief articles used in adulterations are water, sulphuric acid, burnt sugar, acetic and pyroligneous acids, and acrid substances, as chillies and grains of paradise. The water is added to increase its bulk, sulphuric acid and acrid substances to make it pungent and burnt sugar to restore the color lost by dilution. A good deal of the vinegar found at restaurants is simply nothing more than diluted sulphuric acid and water colored with burnt sugar. Occasionally vinegar is found to contain nitric, hydrochloric and tartaric acids, alum, salt, spurge flax, mustard, pellitory and long pepper.

Some factories will not resort to adulterations. They find it pays better to turn out the pure article and they generally command their own prices from consumers, who will have only the best at any cost. If it were an easy matter to detect the impurities in all the vinegars offered for sale, people would not allow themselves to be imposed upon, but insist upon the pure article.

TESTS.—To determine all the ingredients is simply impossible except by a chemical analysis. The presence of sulphuric acid, however, which is a highly injurious substance, may be discovered by dipping a pen in the vinegar and writing with it on paper. If the written words turn black, when dried before the fire, the vinegar is charged with the acid. Or a still more reliable test, add a few drops of the suspected vinegar to a small fragment of cane-sugar and evaporate on the water-bath, heated sand, when the residue will turn more or less black. If mineral acids be present, the color of a paper which has been colored with methylaniline violet, will be destroyed by the mineral in the vinegar, but not by organic acids. If chillies and other acrid substances have been used, evaporate a little of the vinegar on the water-bath and then their presence will be revealed on tasting by the pungent taste.

WHISKEY

Alcohol is the principal constituent of whiskey. Starch, woody fibre, corn, etc., furnish that base, and, were it not for the desirability of imparting speedy age in the product, a good pure article could be secured in the market. But the rivalry and competition between manufacturers has lead to adulterations and the invention of processes, by which to give the article the flavor of age and please the palate of the consumers. Sulphate of copper, sulphuric acid, fusel oil, etc., are some of the delectable(?) ingredients, and a compound is formed, the consumption of which not only steals men's brains, but undermines their constitution and health. Of course the manufacturers throw the blame upon the innocent consumers and assert that if they did not like its taste and consumed it, there would be no occasion for the manufacture of the spurious article. Their argument runs about as follows: ''The fact is, people have become so much accustomed to the taste of compounded liquors that they don't recognize pure liquors when they get it. If they do, they don't like it. Since the process of making 'fine old whiskey' in two days was discovered, a complete revolution in the business has taken place. I know the whole business from beginning to end, and right here let me give you a bit of advice. If you want to drink spirituous liquors, let me tell you the manner in which most of the whiskey now sold is made. The rectifiers add to a barrel of high wines five gallons of the oil of rye. Other essences are put into it to give color and flavor. It is run through the still, purified, placed in barrels and sold. It tastes just as well to the average drinker after two weeks' time as whiskey five years old. The distiller who makes a pure whiskey can't sell it. The consumer doesn't like the taste of pure liquor, because he has not become accustomed to it, and prefers the flavored rectified high wines. The average grade of whiskey costs from 16 cents to 18 cents per gallon to manufacture. The tax is 90 cents per gallon. Say its original cost is $1.10. Now, if a pure liquor is made to become old whiskey it must stand at least five years. The barrel must be open and five or six gallons are lost by evaporation. Consider the loss of interest on the investment for the time the whiskey is standing idle, rents, etc., and you will see that it cannot be sold at a fair profit for less than $4 per gallon. A vast majority, however, of all the 'old' whiskey sold does not bring more than $3 per gallon. The truth is that it is chemically treated and has no real age. The manufacturer is not to blame for compounding liquors. The consumer had rather have it than pay for the genuine article.''

This, however, does not take into consideration the fact that were only the pure kinds of whiskies turned out by the manufacturers, only the pure liquid could and would be consumed. Burnt sugar is also used to give whiskey color and age.

TESTS.—For the detection of fusel oil, a simple practice is to rub some of the spirit between the hands, and after allowing the alcohol to escape, the peculiar odor will be at once perceived. There is no known common method of ascertaining the age of whiskey.

DREGS TURNED INTO WINES.

Pure wines are, as a rule, rare. This is somewhat singular in view of the increased natural production of the article in the United States. The time was not many years since when nearly all the wines were imported from Germany. France, Spain and Hungary, because consumers not only wanted a liquid of good body, strength and boquet, but were possessed of a fanciful idea that the home product was well nigh worthless in comparison with it, but since California, as well as other sections of our country, has fully demonstrated a capacity for its production in large quantities of a better character than that from abroad, affectation for the foreign article has greatly diminished and consumption of the home product increased. The establishment of large wineries, under the charge of professional experts, has largely brought up the reputation of California wines from the reproach placed upon them by the hasty marketing of the first goods. By reason of this reproach in the past, a great deal of the native product has been sold under foreign labels, and some is so still placed upon the market. But the wines of America are now more in favor and in greater demand. The last report of the United States bureau of statistics proves this fact very conclusively. It shows that our total consumption of wines in 1881 was 28,231,106 gallons, of which amount the United States only imported 5,231,106 gallons.

How much of this was pure it is difficult to determine. No statistics are published in this country to indicate the manufacture of wine from other articles than grapes. .In France, however, official reports for 1881 show that no less than 47,000,000 gallons of wine were made from sugar, and 51,000,000 made from raisins, while the imports of Spanish and Italian wines for "blending" amounted to 154,000,000

gallons. These together are equal to one-third of the actual
yield of the French vineyards and strikingly illustrate the
enormous adulterations of French wines. If so great is the
adulteration in France, the land of vineyards, it is safe to say
that only a small percentage of the American wines has been
left unmolested by the dealers. The adulterations are made
with different articles, and made so skillfully as to discount
like efforts of other countries, which largely accounts for the
popularity of American wines. Sometimes different kinds
of grape wines are mixed, and, in other cases, the manufacture is wholly artificial.

The Boston Journal of Chemistry has stated that thousands
of gallons of claret are made by allowing water to soak
through shavings and adding thereto a certain portion of
logwood and tartaric acid, and a little alcohol. It further
stated that good judges could hardly tell the difference between this mixture and the genuine article. Sherries are
often made from cheap white wine, strengthened with brandy,
colored with treacle and flavored with almonds. A kind of
sherry is also manufactured from pale malt and sugar candy,
a small quantity of brandy and inferior wine being added to
flavor it. Sometimes lead is used to restore muddy wines.
White wines are also increased in color by the addition of
caramel or burnt sugar, and red wines by acetic acid. For
flavoring purposes, extract of sweet briar, elderflowers,
arris root, cherry and laurel water are used. Port wine is
made frequently from cider, brandy, elder and damson wines
and a decoction of sloes and powdered catechu, and aged
with a strong decoction of Brazilwood with alum. The
brilliancy of port wine is sometimes increased by means of
alum, and, if turbid, it is cleared by gypsum, while astringency is imparted by oak sawdust. Madeira wines are
adulterated similar to those of sherry and other white wines,
Bordeaux and Burgundy wines are strengthened frequently
by the addition of brandy. Wines are also adulterated with
cane-sugar, the juice of rhubarb, gooseberries, apples and
pears, and colored with elderberry, black sherry, bilberry,
logwood, and Brazilwood, carbonate of soda and potash,

lead, beetroot, aniline dyes, cochineal and sulphuric acid.

Champagne sold in this country is largely spurious. Sometimes it it made of cheap white wine, sugar and coloring matter being added, and then again partly or wholly from gooseberry, apple, pear or rhubarb. In some manufactories, white sugar, whitest brown sugar, crystalline acid or tartaric acid, pure water, white grape wine and brandy in various proportions are used to produce a champagne that sells readily for the genuine. Cider is also employed in the manufacture of a cheap grade of wine. Many American champagnes sold under foreign labels, are simply made from poor grapes and berries. While only a few weeks old, this liquid is bottled green, and pretended age is given by charging it with carbonic acid gas and other slight off-hand preparations, the peculiar effect of which, in connection with this "wine," is to create a rank poison in the human system. Let any doubter make a business of drinking it, and he will soon be convinced. Wine to be good should be made from ripe grapes, after being carefully picked and freed from immature and damaged berries, and then when fermented in bottles, it is as good as the best made in Europe. Sometimes where a red wine is to be produced, quality is sacrificed for color and unripe fruit is used. "The raw wine," says a writer, "is cleared by the use of aluminum, gelatine, and alum, the latter imparting to it great brilliancy, and it is treated with a flavoring syrup which is charged like soda water with carbonic acid, by filling the bottle under a fountain. In this process the wine is liable to be impregnated with lead and copper, which have the effect of disorganizing alike the wine and consumers' stomach. Nausea and headache are among the ill results of drinking 'sparkling wine' thus prepared, or any of the adulterated still wines which are 'doctored' to suit the taste."

Rhine wine is adulterated with sugar, water and spirits. The mixture is fermented with grape husks and then labeled wine.

TESTS.—The wool dyed yellow by means of chromate of potash. Such wool, boiled for some time with genuine wine assumes a characteristic light brown color, no matter in what country the wine is grown; while if the wine be artificially colored with aniline dyes, the wool is dyed red. Wine colored with cochineal does not change the tint of the wool, but extract of Brazil wood gives rise to a dark wine red, and extract of Campeachy wood to a brown or brown black color. A mixture of Campeachy and Brazil wood extract, dyes the wool from iron-grey to black. Wine colored with beetroot can be made colorless by lime water.

All Coliformia grown wines are recognizable to experts by a peculiar flavor, difficult to define, which has been called "earthy," putting one in mind of some of the wines of Burgundy. To most people, however, this peculiarity is not apparent and is not as intense as the "foxy" aroma of wines made from the American grape varieties. Another peculiarity of California wines is that they contain considerable alcohol as the result of the intense sunshine under which the grapes ripen.

If elderberries have been used to color wine, a solution of caustic potash added to it, will produce a purple color; if logwood, a reddish purple; if Brazil wood, a red color; if beetroot, red; and if red mulberries, a purplish color.

The detection of foreign spirit in genuine wine, is exceedingly difficult, even by chemical processes unless the spirit added is very impure. Other substances in wine can only be detected by difficult chemical processes.

BRANDY.

Brandy to be good should be distilled from white and pale red wines. Very little, however, of the article sold in the market is so manufactured. A product that tastes exactly like brandy is very ingeniously turned out and only experts can tell the difference. Of the $70,607,081 worth of the article consumed in the United States in 1881, the largest part is said to have been spurious.

Various processes are used. Some convert corn spirit into imitation brandy by using alcohol, argol, wine-stone, or cream of tartar, acetic ether, French wine vinegar, bruised French plums, flower stuff from cognac, in various proportions, and coloring with burnt sugar to the required tint and roughing it to the taste with a few drops of the tincture of catechu, or Kino; while others use some puncheons of brandy, raisin spirit, tincture of grains of paradise, cherry laurel water and spirit of almond cake, to which they add some quantity of oak sawdust and give color with burnt sugar. Even the French brandy imported into this country, is, either in part or wholly, made from corn, or from molasses, potato or beetroot spirit. British brandy is also spurious, as it is frequently made by the distillation of murk, the name given to the refuse skins and pips of grapes left after the distillation of wine. Since chemistry can produce essential oils artificially—"oils which have the odor of that particular ether to which brandy owes its flavor," foreign countries, alike with America, produce mostly a spurious article. Oak sawdust and tincture of grape stones, purposely prepared, are used to give new brandy the taste of an old spirit. Cayenne pepper is used to give pungency.

TESTS.—The detection of fusel oil may be made by resorting to the process described under the head of "whiskey." If pepper be present, it is recognizable by the irritating character of the vapor given off when the substance containing it is burnt. The rectification of spirits not derived from the grape is so perfect, that their presence is not easily detected in brandy. However by evaporating a portion of the spirit, the presence of a foreign substance may be detected by the peculiar penetrating taste.

GLUCOSE.

Glucose is the cheapest of all sweets. It is manufactured from corn and stands without any special merits of its own. Its sole use is as an adulterant of other sweets and as such derives its commercial value. Its manufacture costs comparatively little. and, when mixed with other forms of saccharine matter, a resulting article is produced that passes for the genuine. It sells to the trade for 4⅛ to 4¼ cents per pound, and the articles it adulterates are sold at a figure far beyond the bounds of commercial honesty. In the case of sugar, except possibly granulated, it is mixed with it to the amount of over one-half and the mixture sells from 9 to 11 cents per pound. A swindle of the most aggravated character! If the price of sugar was reduced proportionate to the use of glucose, the imposition upon the purchaser would not be so great, but the quotations have only fallen some 2 or 3 cents since the growth of glucose manufactories within the last twelve years. Sugar was quoted at 10 to 14 cents per pound in 1870, while at the present time, the market ranges from 7¾ to 11 cents—the decline being due largely to the increased production of sugar at home as well as abroad.

In confectionery the swindle amounts almost to robbery. The price of candy has remained about the same for years and yet glucose is used with it to an enormous extent. Fully 200 per cent. is profit derived chiefly from its use, and when it is taken into account that the sales of the confectioners of Chicago alone reach annually over a million dollars, it can readily be seen that the business is a most profitable one. In syrup, honey and maple sugar, it also enters very largely as an adulterant and brings the dealers handsome returns.

At the present time, there are manufactories in operation in Buffalo, N. Y.; Glen Cove, N. Y.; St. Louis, Mo.; Detroit, Mich.; Des Moines, Iowa City and Davenport. Iowa; Tippecanoe, Peoria, Freeport and Geneva, Ill., and an immense establishment, with a capacity of 15,000 bushels of corn per day, is about completed in Chicago. With a view of controlling the market, they all belong to a general association, which fixes prices and limits production. Besides regulating the trade, they speculate on their own hook with syrup ‘‘doctored’’ by themselves and sell at a figure the same as that for the pure article. To sell at less figures would be an admission of adulteration and purchasers would be placed on their guard. Quotations are therefore kept up both for the sake of gain and to deceive the people.

Of course in this game of general grab, they are not slow to make all the money possible out of their business and resort to adulterations of the very article, which has its existence simply as an adulterant of other articles. The dealer in swindling his customers is thus himself unconsciously being swindled. When he buys the glucose he supposes it to be real glucose, but if he possessed the knowledge of thorough analysis, he would find that the manufacturers mix with it, by a certain process, the lowest form of other saccharine matter in order to enhance its sweetness. There is thus a Pelion on Ossa of fraud, and the consumer of sweets is at the mercy of both the greedy manufacturers and the dealers.

Whether glucose is injurious to the system, doctors are divided in opinion. Some maintain that it is highly detrimental to health, while others insist that it is perfectly harmless.

TESTS.—As glucose is a sugar less soluble and sweeter than cane-sugar, the suspected article may be placed in a goblet of water and after stirring for some time, what fails to become speedily assimilated with the water may be set down as glucose from its crystalline appearance.

TOBACCO.

Tobacco is used more extensively than any other stimulant or narcotic. It has been estimated by Dr. Geo. M. Beard, of the New York University, that it is used by 900,000,000 of the human race and that over four billion pounds are raised annually throughout the world, which is nearly four pounds a year for every man, woman and child upon the face of the globe.

Whether in the form of smoking or chewing tobacco or snuff, it is of course outrageously adulterated. The leaf, when rolled up for chewing purposes, is treated with molasses and some gritty substances to give taste and weight, and where a cheap article is desired, the leaf, stock and refuse that accumulates from month to month in the factories are put together and a fine wrapper placed around each plug. When it is considered that the refuse has been trod upon by dirty boots or shoes and saturated with the saliva of the workingmen, it can readily be imagined what an excellent chewing compound has been formed.

Cigars are made from inferior leaves, highly flavored and the narcotic properties heightened by chemical processes, and, in some instances, cherry leaves, specially prepared, are mixed with the better qualities of the weed. Some brands have wrappers made out of paper manufactured and colored in imitation of the leaf.

Before the perfection of the art of deception, it was an easy matter to determine a good cigar by the light brown specks on it. These were made by worms, and as they would only touch the best tobacco, smokers would select such cigars as were thus marked. Chemists, who are now a part of every well established manufactory, found a way of imitating these spots, and that circumvented the test. The ashes were also a good indication. If white, the cigar was good;

if not, then it was bad. The chemists again came to the
rescue and made so-called "cabbage leaves"—the reputed
use of which with tobacco is a pure fiction—burn as white as
the best kind of tobacco. Ammonia is largely used for this
purpose, although sometimes the same end is attained by
soaking the tobacco in a strong solution of saltpetre. The
latter practice is said to be very injurious to consumers. In
order to give cigars an intoxicating quality, some manufacturers dip the fillings into a solution of sulphuric ether
and bromide of potassium, which is pronounced to be highly
injurious. The peculiar effects of some cigars are said to be
unquestionably due to their being filled up with so-called
nervines, narcotics and stimulants. Some flavor their cigars
with a combination of vanilla, valerian and New England
rum. Other substances are also used for flavoring, such as
opium, the tonka bean, balsam of fir, cedar oil and ascarilla
bark.

Snuff is adulterated with pepper and other substances that
give it weight, pungency and color.

TESTS.—There is no reliable test except one's experience
in the use of tobacco. A close inspection of plug tobacco
will reveal its impurities, and smokers of cigars can determine between a natural and artificial flavor. A fine cigar
can hardly be said to improve by manipulations beyond the
necessary curing and should burn evenly and well for some
time, without the presence of any hard or crumbling particles.
The wrapper should have a smooth, clear surface, and the
ends present a filling of leaves of fine fiber, loosely rolled
together and not compactly pressed as if solid. Poor leaves
crumble and are easily pressed together, and when burned,
burn somewhat like a rolled mass of rags.

SODA WATER, GINGER BEER AND MINERAL WATER.

GAS MAKES THEM ALL BUBBLE ALIKE.

Nearly all the soda water, ginger beer and mineral water sold are not by any means what their names imply. The mineral water, in which the greatest efficacy has been found, is that which has been imported, and the demand for it has been so great that chemists have found processes for manufacturing water that tastes exactly like it. Foreign as well as home dealers have turned out the spurious article, and so great has been the competition that a government tax on the imported article came to the assistance of the home manufacturers. Genuine mineral waters, although exempt from duty, suffered alike with the rest, but recently the government decided upon admitting it free to our ports, where it could be conclusively shown that it was natural mineral water impregnated with its own gas. Some of the so-called mineral water is simply made with powdered effervescent salts, which are put up and sold by druggists in bottles containing two and four ounces each. In charging a fountain, six ounces of the powder is used for every ten gallons of water, and where a draught is prepared extemporaneously, half a teaspoonful of the powder is placed in a goblet previous to filling with water.

Soda water, in order to be such, should contain alkali, but the kind sold in the market is simply water impregnated with carbonic acid gas, not a particle of soda being used. In like manner ginger beer should be made of ginger, sugar and water subjected to fermentation.

TESTS.—The presence of the right ingredients can only be determined by chemistry. On standing, however, exposed to the air for some time the liquids lose their strength and become insipid, whereas the genuine keep their strength and body for a considerable time.

BREAD.

One would suppose that the bakers would be above any tricks of adulterations. But it appears not. The moment he commences his dough until he puts his loaf up for sale, he smuggles into it articles calculated to increase the weight and deceive the public. Water is cheap, and hence his desire that his bread should contain as much of it as possible. He accordingly soaks it with all the water it will hold and then rushes it into a hot oven with as little delay as possible. This produces a crust instantaneously and prevents the escape of water. He next covers his bread with cloths and thereby keeps it moist until it is sold. If he is especially avaricious he adds some rice, and this, when cooked, swells up greatly and absorbs a great deal of water. Potatoes are added for a similar purpose. He also uses alum to give his bread a white appearance. Sulphate of copper is sometimes used for the same purpose.

Alum hardens the nutritious qualities of the bread and renders digestion difficult. Besides, sometimes it is used to "doctor up" damaged flour. Bread made at home is darker than baker's, for the reason that no injurious alum is used. The whiter the bread, the greater the adulteration either with alum, or sulphate of alumina and potash.

TESTS.—What has already been stated as to color is an indication of adulteration. When soaked in water, home-made bread in which pure yeast has been used, does not present as spongy an appearance as the adulterated bread. Or immerse a slice of bread in a decoction of logwood, when the presence of alum will be indicated by the appearance of a blue coloration.

BAKING POWDERS.

The market is filled with patent baking powders. Country fairs are overrun with their exhibition and city stores are filled with placards advertising their merits. In some places, bread and biscuits, freshly made, are parceled out to customers to show what light, white, airy and palatable products can be raised from them. Most of these powders are made of alum and bicarbonate of soda with some starch or flour. The city chemist of Chicago pronounces them very objectionable and maintains that alum, whatever condition it may be converted into in the bread-baking, becomes in the stomach, altered into aluminic chloride, a styptic, or astringent much more powerful than alum itself. Powders are also made with carbonate of soda and tartaric acid, which are objectionable since the resulting tartarate of soda possesses aperient properties. Most baking powders so-called are made of about three parts of starch, one part bicarbonate of soda and one part alum. The presence of alum is noticeable in nearly all samples, and its use for this purpose has been invariably condemned by the medical profession.

TESTS.—There is no reliable or easy test except by chemical analysis.

CREAM OF TARTAR.

AN ARTICLE USED EXTENSIVELY IN COOKING.

The house committee on commerce, in its investigations into certain few adulterations recently, submitted to congress a report, from which we take the following in reference to the subject under consideration :

"Commercial cream of tartar contains tartarate of lime, which must, within limits, be accepted as natural to it. Cases have recently been tried in England in which the adulteration charged was the lime tartarate present in this salt, but the magistrate properly refused to convict. Yet this is an article which is subject to gross adulteration. Among eighteen samples examined by the experts, six were found to be of satisfactory purity, eleven of them contained lime varying from 17 to 90 per cent., three of them having nearly the latter figure. Two contained no cream of tartar at all, but consisted, the one of sulphate of lime, alum, and acid phosphate of lime, and the other of alum, acid phosphate, and potato-starch. Corn-starch was also found in large proportion in one of the lime sulphate powders. Considering the use of cream of tartar in cooking, its impure condition is a serious evil. As we all know, this article enters into the manufacture of bread of the world, and certainly such adulterations should be, if possible, stopped. Of nine samples examined in New York one had 80 per cent. of terra-alba, one 61 per cent., and the others contained lime-salt."

TESTS.—For terra alba, dissolve in a solution of caustic potash, which leaves the impurity undissolved. For lime in any form, dissolve in aqua ammonia and add a little solution of oxalate of ammonia, which will precipitate chalk or lime in any form. For starch or flour, test the solution with iodine, which will give a blue color.

CIDER..

In a country abounding with orchards and cider presses, it would seem that there ought to be no occasion for a spurious article, and yet we find it in the very center of a cider producing section. In fact, cider has been so skillfully adulterated that it is difficult to tell the false from the genuine. Sometimes the pure juice is mixed with water and then brought up to the right flavor with either acetic or carbonic acid. In most cases, however, water is sweetened with sugar, impregnated with tartaric acid and colored with burnt sugar. This is the kind mainly sold in large cities. As bottled cider is liable to become impure, sulphate of soda and other chemicals are mixed with it to keep it sweet. The difficulty of getting pure, hard cider is very unfortunate, as it is regarded by physicians a most valuable beverage for the nervous and dyspeptic. Dr. Beard calls it "the Rhine wine of America" and adds that it would be "better, far better for our American ladies if they took more hard cider and less tea and coffee. It clears the digestion, corrects the liver and sharpens the appetite."

TESTS.—By exposing the mixture for some moments to the air, the gas escapes and a flat, insipid tasting fluid remains, having little of the body and pungency of pure cider.

CHICCORY.

THE ROOT OF CONSIDERABLE EVIL.

This plant is very extensively cultivated throughout the country. Its value lies in the use of its roots, which form, when duly prepared, a leading admixture to coffee, as already shown. The roots grow deep into the ground and are taken up just before the plant blossoms in August or September. They are then washed, kiln-dryed and roasted, after which a very small quantity of lard is added to improve the appearance of the powder. This powder strikingly resembles ground coffee and cannot be easily detected from it by the naked eye. Hence the great temptation to mix it with coffee and produce an article, on which large profits can be realized, especially since the plant is raised with scarcely any trouble and is prepared at a very trifling expense. Once it grew in a natural state without any merits being discovered in it, but now its cultivation has assumed large proportions to meet the demand and greed of unscrupulous merchants. So well has it been prepared for the market that it not only supplies the home demand, but large quantities have been shipped to Europe, where it has achieved a reputation as being superior to the native product.

Not satisfied with its cheapness as an adulterant, the dealers in coffee mix with the chiccory different kinds of roasted corn, as wheat and rye, beans, acorns, carrots, beet-root, burnt sugar and red earths, and thus greatly enhance the pecuniary value of packages labeled "pure coffee" and swell their own ill-gotten bank accounts. Sometimes the seeds of wild senna are mixed with it,. and, as their odor closely resembles roasted coffee, the resulting article is made still more deceptive.

TESTS.—The microscope will reveal the different articles used by the difference in their cellular structures. In a mixed article, the chiccory will be made manifest by the particles swelling up on the addition of water, and the other ingredients will show scarcely any change.

FLOUR.

The adulteration of flour is not carried on to as great an extent as with other articles of commerce. The millers, as a general rule, run it into barrels as it comes from the grindstone and ship it to the market. When it reaches the centers of trade and has remained stored for awhile, under unfavorable conditions, it is liable to be damaged and then the sellers usually mix with it alum and carbonate of soda to stop decomposition and correct the acidity arising therefrom, thus making it a more salable article. Of course, in some instances, unscrupulous persons add chalk, mineral white, rice, beans, corn and potato flour to give the article bulk and weight and so enable them to realize greater profits.

TESTS.—The only way to detect the adulteration of flour with other kinds of flour is by the use of the microscope.

CHOCOLATE.

Chocolate, which is the prepared state of Cocoa for use, has been designated as a food fit for the gods. The distinction is appropriate for its infusion graces, for the most part, the tables of the rich and well-to-do people. It is produced in Mexico, the West Indies, Central America and on the French Island of Bourbon. Altough it is a great luxury in its pure state, taste is sacrificed to the greed of dealers, and so it is found frequently adulterated with various flours, chicory root, colored ferruginous earths, corn, sago meal, tapioca, arrowroot, potato starch, sugar, cocoa-nut oil, lard and tallow. Even the finest chocolate is made up with clarified mutton-suet and common sugar with cocoa. For color, carbonate of lime, hydrated sulphate of lime, red ochre, Venetian red, umber and clay are used.

TESTS.—To detect adulterations proceed as follows: "If in breaking chocolate, it is gravelly; if it melt in the mouth without leaving a cool, refreshing taste; if on addition of hot water, it becomes thick and pasty, and, lastly, if it form a gelatinous mass on cooking, it is adulterated with starch and such like substances.

Where earthy and other solid substances are deposited from chocolate mixed with water, either the cocoa beans have not been well cleansed, inferior sugar has been employed, or mineral subtances have been added to it, eithei for the purpose of coloring or of increasing its weight. Moreover, when chocolate has a kind of cheesy taste, animal tat has been added ; and when very rancid, either vegetable oil or even the seeds themselves have been employed."

PICKLES.

The pickling industry has received a great impetus within the past few years. The supply has generally come from abroad, but since improved methods have been discovered for preserving fruits and vegetables, farmers have found it quite profitable to cultivate their growth. Pickling factories now abound all over the country, and were it not for the substances used to give color, there would be no danger in eating pickles. Whenever articles are pickled in the right manner, they are usually of a yellow color rather than green. The articles, however, when presented in the market, present a vivid bluish green color, more intense than that of the fresh vegetables. When therefore they are of decided green, they nearly always contain copper, but when they are of a yellowish or brownish green, copper is never present. The manufacturers, however, desire their wares to present a fresh color so as to please the eye of the consumers and prove more salable. Whenever therefore they prepare the vegetables, they boil them either with copper at the bottom of the pot, or allow them to stand in a copper pan for twenty-four hours.

TESTS.—The presence of copper in pickles, bottled fruits nd vegetables i s thus clearly indicated by their color.

MEAT.

Poor is the family that cannot afford a plate of meat once a day at least. In Europe, the article is a rare luxury with the poorer classes, and only graces their tables on festal occasions, but in America, where it can be had in abundance and at a small cost, it forms the leading dish at two, if not the three, meals of a day throughout the year,

If it were not that unscrupulous dealers palmed off on the unsuspecting people unsound and unwholesome meat, very little fault could be found with the trade. Very often dealers find it to their profit to sell meat not acceptable to a first-class market. They purchase it at a low figure, and by treatment present it in such a condition as to make it readily pass with a certain class of consumers as a first-class article.

Where so many thousand heads of cattle, hogs and sheep are daily received and slaughtered in a large city like Chicago, it follows that a good many are diseased. Among the number many also die in transit, and, as their sale to rendering establishments would bring very little, they are clandestinly sold to sharp speculators at a saving price on original cost Again the meat of an old one is sometimes sold as that of a young animal. It is said that it is not easy to determine the age of an animal when living and still more difficult to do so when dead. The age is generally ascertained by the teeth and horns, but as butchers and owners of meat markets do not exhibit meat "on the hoof," the consumer has only general means of posting himself as to its real character. As to veal, he is entirely at the mercy of the dealers. He trusts to their honesty as to whether it is of the proper maturity, but he is often mislead by their greed and rapacity. It is asserted by good authorities that no less than five hundred calves are daily shipped to Chicago, and that out of that number a large portion are calves only a day or so old. They are bought at a low figure and sold at a considerable advance. Veal has therefore been banished from the tables of those who have become cognizant of the practice.

TESTS.—Meat, when fresh, has certain well defined and easily recognized characteristics. The muscles of sound flesh should be firm, elastic, pale for the young animal, and darker colored for the old one, and when cut across a little reddish juice should flow out for some time. The flesh when of a deep purple tint is an indication that the animal has not been slaughtered, but has died without being bled. Diseased meat has a sickly, corpse-like smell. Bad meat is wet and flabby, with fat looking like jelly. The fat should be firm and without being marked with blood spots. As meat decays, the fibres become paler or even turn greenish. In boiling or roasting, bad meat looses in quality and becomes hard. If a clean knife is pushed up to the hilt, the resistance will be uniform in good meat, while in putrefying meat some parts are softer than others. The smell of the knife is also a good test. Twenty-four hours after killing, the marrow of the hind legs is of a light rosy red color and moderately firm, if the animal has been a healthy one, but if it is soft, brownish or exhibits black points the animal has been sick or putrefaction has set in.

Still further, good meat has the following characteristics: "Beef should be of a bright red color, well streaked with yellow fat, and surrounded with a thick outside layer of fat. Veal and pork should be of a bright flesh color, with an abundance of hard, white, semi-transparent fat. Lamb of the best kind has delicate rosy meat, and white, almost transparent fat. Fresh poultry may be known by its full, bright eyes, pliable feet and moist skin ; the best is plump, fat and nearly white. The feet and neck of a chicken suitable for broiling are large in proportion to its size ; the tip of the breast-bone is soft and easily bent between the fingers. Fish when fresh, have firm flesh, bright clear eyes, rigid fins and ruddy gills. Lobsters and crabs must be bright in color and lively in movement.''

VARIETY IS THE SPICE OF LIFE.

MUSTARD.—The common adulterations of mustard are with wheat flour or meal and colored with turmeric and sometimes with chrome yellow. Other adulterations practiced are those with cayenne pepper, ginger, charlock, ground rice, silicate of alumina or clay and chromate of lead. The pepper is used to give pungency to the mustard and the clay or other mineral substances for bulk and weight. Chrome yellow and lead are dangerous admixtures. The microscope is the best test for flour or meal. For ascertaining lead or chrome yellow, take a sample of the mustard to a drug store and have added to the watery mixture of the suspected article, dilute muriatic acid until it shows a clear reaction on litmus paper, then drop in a few grains of sulphuret of potassium, which will give the mixture a reddish brown tint if lead is present and leave it unchanged if it is free. A still more positive test is to pass sulphureted hydrogen through the mixture. For evidence of turmeric coloring, use a solution of borax, which gives a dark brown color with turmeric. Turmeric is for concealing the harmless adulteration with flour or meal, which reduces the strength and cheapens the goods with no damage except to the consumer's purse.

FARINACEOUS FOODS.— Nearly all are simple compounds. In some cases, wheat flour, slightly baked, sweetened with sugar, together with potato starch, Indian corn meal and tapioca are used; in other cases, simply gluten of wheat with a proportion of wheat starch; in still others, nothing but potato flour, artificially colored and, lastly, wheat flour, tartaric acid and carbonate of soda. These articles make up the foods with high sounding titles and in flaming colored labels.

SAGO.—This substance is obtained from the pith of the stems of several kinds of palm, which grow on the islands of the Indian Archipelago, in Madagascar, New Guinea, China and Japan by a peculiar process. The leading adulteration of sago flour and of granulated sago is with potato starch. Frequently the false sago prepared from potato starch is substituted for true sago. The microscope can alone detect the adulterations.

TAPIOCA.—This root is cultivated in South America, from which after due process, Cassava meal or bread is made and a juice extracted that after a time deposits a farina or starch, which is called tapioca meal. This meal being dried constitutes granular tapioca. The adulterations of tapioca are with mixtures of other starches as those of sago and potato. With the microscope their detection is easy and certain.

ALLSPICE.—This article is the berry or fruit of a tree, which grows in the West Indies and in Jamaica. Its chief adulterations are with mustard husk, bread-crust, beans, corn-starch, woody tissues and turmeric, and can be detected with the microscope.

MIXED SPICE.—This is a mixture in different proportions of several spices, as ground ginger, allspice or pimento with cassia or cinnamon and a small quantity of powdered cloves. Wheat flour, ground rice, sago and potato flour are used chiefly for adulterations.

ANCHOVIES.—Several kinds of fish are substituted for or mixed with the genuine Gorgona anchovy. The chief of these are Dutch, French, Sicilian fish and sardines and sprats. Besides, the brine, in which the fish are preserved, is highly colored with bole Armenian and Venetian red. An expert who is familiar with the flesh of the different fishes can only detect the adulterations.

CAYENNE PEPPER.—Cayenne pepper is subjected to very general adulterations. Red lead, sulphuret of mercury, ground rice, turmeric, red earths, husk of white mustard seed are used for this purpose. The use of red lead and and other red coloring matter is to conceal other adulterations and to preserve the color of the Cayenne. Salt is employed to give weight. To detect foreign substances use the microscope.

NUTMEGS.—Nutmegs are sometimes mixed with riddled nuts, eaten by insects, the small apertures are then closed with a kind of cement formed of flour, oil and some powder of nutmegs. These may be discovered by soaking them in water. Also prick them with a pin. If they are good, the oil will instantly spread around the puncture.

POWDERED CLOVES AND CINNAMON are also adulterated. The microscope will reveal the ingredients.

GINGER.—To improve the color of ginger, it is frequently rubbed over with lime, and in some cases, washed in chalk and water. The adulterations are with sago meal, tapioca, potato flour, wheat flour, ground rice, cayenne pepper, mustard husks and turmeric powder. The microscope will reveal the foreign substances.

PEPPER.—The adulterations of pepper are made with linseed meal, mustard husk, wheat flour, pea flour, sago, rice flour and pepper dust. To which may be added wheat bran, sulphate of lime and rape seed, etc. "Out of four samples examined," says the report of the congressional committee, "taken from respectable houses in the City of New York, only one was found pure. The others contained baked flour and rye, with sand enough to prove the unclean condition of the peppers when milled. Dr. Hassel in 1855 reported forty-three specimens taken from English stores, sixteen of which were adulterated. The chemist of the National Board of Health gave the results of a larger experience. Of 1,116 peppers, 576 were adulterated with rice, sago, potato starch, brown and white mustard, wood, wheat bran and flour, oat flour, and ground gypsum. The Commissary-General supplid sixteen unopened sample cans for investigation. Of these two were adulterated with fresh flour, while six showed, from the quantity of sand present, the unclean and probably inferior quality of the peppers. Of thirty-two samples which were purchased four were pure. The remaining twenty-eight samples were mixed with ingredients which weakened their strength and impaired their usefulness." The adulterations can be discovered by the use of the microscope.

LIQUORICE.—The principal adulterations are those with

sugar and chalk. On boiling, the sugar and chalk will become assimilated with the water, and liquorice settle at the bottom.

ANNATTO.—This article, which is used foi coloring, is itself subject to adulteration. It is mixed with sulphate of lime, carbonate of lime, salt, alkali, red lead and copper and ferruginous earths.

CURRY POWDERS.—The genuine powder is composed of turmeric, black pepper, corriander seeds, cayenne, fenugreek, cardamons, cumin, ginger, allspice and cloves. Of these turmeric forms the largest proportions. Its adulterations are with ground rice, potato starch, salt and red lead.

SAUCES, POTTED MEATS AND FISH.—These are colored with red ferruginous earths, as bole Armenian and Venetian red.

SYRUP.—This is largely adulterated with cheap glucose. The manufacturers of glucose buy large quantities of sugar syrup and in consequence of it, the price of the pure article advanced, within three months, 15 to 18 cents.

SODA SYRUPS.—The syrups used with the soda drawn from fountains are abominations of the worst kind. Raspberry, strawberry, pine-apple, lemon, etc., are no more related to the substances from which they derive their names than opium is related to food. They are made up from various chemicals to give them a flavor of the genuine article, and those who use these "extracts" regularly find to their regret that the stomach determines their quality better than the palate. They are poisonous in their character and should be used very sparingly if at all. Good drug firms furnish the best quality

MAPLE SUGAR is adulterated with muscovado and brown sugars. In some cases, only sufficient maple is retained to impart a flavor to the mixed article.

GRAIN.—In order to raise the grade and improve the quality of poor or damaged wheat, barley and other grains, they are subjected to fumigation by sulphur and placed upon the market as sound and in their natural condition.

RUM is a spirit obtained from fermented skimmings of the

juice of sugar-cane mixed with molasses and lees and diluted with water. It is adulterated with cayenne or coculus indicus to give it strength, sugar and burnt sugar to restore sweetness and color. As it has a tendency to create prespiration, it is used frequently by persons to break up a cold.

GIN is made from unmalted rye and barley malt, rectified with juniper berries. It is also made from malt and barley, molasses and corn flavored with juniper berries and sometimes improved with corriander, cardamon and caraway seeds, grains of paradise, almond cake and orange peel. It is adulterated with alum, carbonate of potash, acetate of lead, sulphuric acid, and sulphate of zinc.

RANCIDITY OF FATS.—A test for rancidity of fats is to mix with them iodide of potassium, which, if in the least affected, quickly assume an orange color, the tint being directly proportionate to the amount of rancidity.

INJURIOUS SUBSTANCES.

THE POISONOUS STUFF THAT ONE SWALLOWS.

The following substances are pronounced to be very highly injurious by Dr. A. H. Hassell, of England:

Coculus indicus, very poisonous.

Arsenite of copper, emerald green or Scheel's green.

Sulphate of copper, or blue vitriol, and acetate of copper or verdigris.

Carbonate of copper or verditer.

The three chromates of lead.

Red oxide of lead.

Red ferruginous earths, as Venetian red, bole Armenian, red and yellow ochres, umber. etc.

Carbonate of lead.

Plumbago, or black lead.

Bisulphuret of mercury, or cinnabar.

Sulphate of iron.

Cayenne.

Picric acid, in doses of 1 to 10 grains many animals can be killed.

The three false Brunswick greens, being mixtures of the chromates of lead and indigo, or Prussian blue.

Oxychlorides of copper, or true Brunswick greens.

Orpiment, or sulphuret of arsenicum.

Ferrocyanide of iron, or Prussian blue.

Antwerp blue and chalk.

Indigo.

Ultramarine.

Artificial ultramarine.

Hydrated sulphate of lime, mineral white or plaster of Paris.

Alum.

Sulphuric acid.

Bronze powders, or alloys of copper and zinc.

Chromates of potash.

Gamboge.

COLORS IN CONFECTIONERY.
PIGMENTS THAT ARE THE FIGMENTS OF SHARPERS.

List of colors that should be excluded from confectionery
on the ground that they are very injurious to health :

YELLOW COLOR.—Gamboge; the three chrome yellows, or
chromate of lead; massicot, or protoxide of lead; yellow
orpiment, or sulphuret of arsenicum; King's yellow, or sulphuret of arsenicum with lime and sulphur; iodide of lead;
sulphuret of antimony; yellow ochre.

RED COLOR.—Red lead, minium, or red oxide of lead;
vermilion, or bisulphuret of mercury; red orpiment, realger,
or bisulphuret of arsenic; iodide of mercury; red ferruginous
earths, or Venetian red, etc.

BROWN COLOR.—Vandyke brown and umber.

PURPLE COLOR.—All purples resulting from the mixture
of any of the reds or blues given.

BLUE COLOR.—Prussian blue, or ferrocyanide of iron;
indigo; Antwerp blue, a preparation of Prussian blue; cobalt;
smalt, a glass of cobalt; blue verditer, or sesquicarbonate
of copper; ultramarine, a double silicate of alumina and
soda, with sulphuret of sodium; German or artificial ultramarine, which resembles in its composition natural ultramarine.

GREEN COLOR.—The three false Brunswick greens, being
mixtures of lead and indigo; mineral green, green verditer
or subcarbonate of copper: verdigris, or diocetate of copper;
Emerald green, or arsenite of copper; the true Brunswick
greens, or oxychlorides of copper; false verditer, or sulphuret of copper and chalk.

VARIOUS BRONZE POWDERS.—Gold, silver and copper
bronzes; these consist of alloys, in different proportions of
copper and zinc, white lead or carbonate of lead.

The use of the above colors in candies, etc., is rigidly pro-
hibited by the Department of Health in France.   Since the

list was put in force, a number of colors are now prepared from coal tar, every tint being imitated. If these dyes, including aniline dyes, were pure, their use, it is stated, would be comparatively harmless, but being frequently contaminated with arsenic, they ought to be condemned. How extensively arsenic is used is indicated by "Food and Health," of New York, which says: "We import annually 2,000,000 pounds of this deadly poison—one cent's worth of which would kill 2,800 people—and the bulk of this import is used in the preparation of food and clothing."

THE PURPOSES SOME ARTICLES SERVE.

BULK, WEIGHT, COLOR, TASTE, SMELL, etc.

The following is a list of substances used for different purposes of adulteration as set forth:

FOR BULK AND WEIGHT.

Acorns,
Arrowroot,
Apples,
Almonds, milk of,
Corn, Indian,
Curd,
Cassia,
Charlock,
Cake, ground oil,
Earths, red ferruginous,
Gelatine,
Gum,
Hawthorn, leaves of,
Lime, hydrated sulphate of,
Liver, baked,
Mangel-wurzel,
Magnesia,
Oat-meal,
Plane, leaves of,
Parsnip,
Rice,
Starch,
Suet, mutton,
Seeds, radish,
Turmeric,
Turnip, pulp of,

Barley,
Beans,
Beetroot,
Brains, sheep's and calves'.
Chiccory,
Carrots,
Chalk,
Cider,
Dextrin,
Elm, leaves of,
Fats, animal,
Glucose,
Ginger,
Iron, magnetic oxide of,
Leaves, various kinds,
Lard,
Mustard husks,
Marble, powdered,
Potatoes,
Pea-flour,
Pipe-clay,
Salt,
Sawdust,
Seeds, mustard,
Sloe, leaves of,
Tapioca,
Tea, exhausted

Beach, leaves of,
Bonedust,
Biscuit, roasted,
Clave-stalks, powdered,
Chestnut, horse,
Clay, different varieties,
Flours, roasted wheat & rye, potato, rice, peas, etc.,
Grounds, coffee,
Lead, red,
Linseed meal,
Lie-tea,
Lime, carbonates of,
Lime, sulphate of,
Maize,
Oak, leaves of,
Pepper dust,
Plaster of Paris,
Rye,
Sago,
Sugar,
Sand,
Soda,
Treacle,
Tan, oak-bark,

Tallow,
Water,
White Potter's Clay.

leaves of,
Woody-fibre,

Wheat.
Willow, leaves of,

FOR COLOR.

Annatto.
Alkali,
Brazil-wood,
Cochineal,
Chinese yellow,
Cherries,
Cobalt,
Gamboge,
Greens, the three
  Brunswick,
Lead, red and black,
Litmus,
Lime, sulphate of,
Mallow flowers,
Naples yellow,
Ochre, red,
Red, Indian,
Dutch Pink,
Sugar, burnt,
Turmeric,
Umber,
Vandyke brown,
Yellow dyes,

Antwerpblue,
Alum,
Bole Armenian,
Carbonate of cop-
  per,
China clay,
Potash,
Green, Emerald,
Indian red,
Lake,
Lead, chromate of,
Liver, baked,
Mica,
Mercury, bisul-
  phuret of,
Plumbago,
Red, Venetian,
Salt,
Soap-stone,
Treacle,
Vermilion,
Vegetable red,
Yellow ochre.

Aniline dyes,
Black cherries,
Black lead,
Copper, salts of,
Chrome yellow,
Chalk,
Earths, red ferru-
  ginous,
Indigo,
Lead, carbonate of.
Liquorice,
Logwood, decoction
  of,
Madder root,
Orange,
Prussian blue,
Rose Pink,
Sienna,
Smalt,
Ultramarine, arti-
  ficial,
White lead,

FOR TASTE, SMELL AND OTHER PROPERTIES.

Alum,
Angelica root,
Acetic acid,
Cassia,
Cardamon seeds,
Catechu,
Coculus indicus,
Cream of tartar,
Grains of Paradise,
Gin flavorings,

Artificial essences,
Almond cake,
Burnt sugar,
Cayenne,
Caustic lime,
Camomile,
Coriander seeds,
Earths, red ferru-
  ginous,
Gentian,

Acetate of amyl,
Arsenic,
Butyrate of amyl,
Copper, sulphate of,
Cinnamon,
Carbonates of soda
  and potash,
Emerald green,
Ginger,
Grey salts,

Gum,
Iron, sulphate of,
Lead, acetate of,
Orange peel,
Oyster shells,
Oil of turpentine,
Picric acid,
Quassia,
Sage,
Sulphuric acid,
Treacle,
Wormwood.

Honey,
Lime, caustic,
Long pepper,
Oil of almonds,
Orange powder,
Opium,
Potash, carbonate
    of,
Sugar,
Sulphate of potash,
Tartaric acid,

Hydrochloric acid,
Liquorice,
Mustard seed,
Orris root,
Oak sawdust,
Powder, Chinese Bo-
    tanical,
Salt,
Soda, carbonate of,
Salt of tartar,
White salts,

THE LEGAL AND MORAL ASPECTS OF THE CASE.
WHAT OUGHT TO BE DONE TO SUPPRESS ADULTERATIONS.

In the foregoing pages, we have set forth the adulterations of the leading articles of diet and stimulants. They form, however, only a small portion of the deceptions practiced in business. Were the whole field covered, the exposition of the frauds would fill a good sized volume and prove appalling by their extent and enormity.

In the drug line alone, the adulterations of goods are practiced almost beyond the bounds of belief, and put to blush the manipulators of food by their superlative fineness. Drugs are designed to improve and strengthen the vital forces, and their manufacture and compounding should therefore be of the best and purest character. Here at least there ought to be no trifling with the human system. But such is not the case. In the balance, the greed for gain overbalances the side of humanity. Health is sacrificed for wealth.

A wholesale drug firm in Chicago has shown, in a private work of their own for circulation among their customers, a list of some adulterations, but this list is meager and incomplete and seems to be merely supplementary to a pharmaceutical book, which was published some three years ago and which gave chemical formulae for detecting adulterations in drugs. In spite of this exposure, dealers in the wholesale line seem to have not only continued their practices, but enlarged upon the number of articles susceptible to sophistication. How extensively has grown this practice may be judged by the following, taken from a circular issued recently by a firm of manufacturing chemists of Peoria: "We have assumed that the jobbing trade are, as a rule, handling and selling adulterated powdered drugs. Of this we have the most abundant evidence, having carefully examined many samples obtained from jobbers, with the object of finding out exactly what kind of goods we were obliged to compete with, and we regret to say, that we have yet to find a pure sample of bulk goods. We do not say all the goods offered are adulterated, but that all we have examined are."

Deception, however, is not alone confined to foods and drugs, but extends to perfumery, the manufacture of clothing and other industries. In machinery, manufacturers reconstruct machines and boilers from pieces taken out of old ones and palm them off as new, and, in fabrics, shoddy material is used to make up what appears to be good, durable goods. In perfumery, very few scents are made directly from the flowers, the names of which they bear, but from beef fat, lard, etc., exposed to fresh flowers in close boxes until thoroughly charged with their odors, from which fifty or more combinations of the odors of other flowers are made. Perfumes of other kinds are made from essential oils and not from what they are supposed to be manufactured. Standard fertilizers, such as guanos, superphosphates, etc., are also adulterated. Their sales aggregate millions of dollars annually, and, because of the large quantities purchased, the tillers of the soil are unconsciously deceived.

"Is there no remedy for this wholesale and almost universal deception?" will be asked. In some classes of articles there is, but in a majority of cases there is not the slightest protection at law. In England, the consumers are measurably protected by "The Sale of Food and Drugs Act," adopted in 1860 and amended by parliament in 1875, and under its provisions aggrieved parties can not only secure redress, but involve the adulterating tradesmen in severe penalties. In France, the law prosecutes as an adulteration all chemical coloring of wines and prescribes certain articles that must not be "handled." In Germany also, adulteration of some articles is made a punishable offense.

In the United States, there is no national law touching adulterations. Congress recently investigated the question, but so far it has taken no action except to receive a report of its committee. Several states and some cities have taken the matter in hand, but the laws adopted have only had reference to some special article or articles. In Michigan, the legislature passed a law against the adulteration of honey and some other articles, but failed to cover the whole field. In Chicago, the city council adopted an ordinance looking to the suppression of spurious butter, but failed to cover other branches. In New York, a bill to prohibit the coloring of oleomargarine to give it the appearance of butter was defeated this year by the legislature in the interest of the manufacturers, but no other kindred adulterations were presented for action.

Among all the states of the union, Illinois, however, is an exception. It has almost complete legislation on adulterations. It has covered food, drink and medicine, and presented very comprehensive and forcible acts touching their sophistication. But after all, these acts are deficient in one particular. They do not provide for a central, active and responsible authority. In the case of the drug act, its chief defect is that instead of entrusting the duty of ferreting out and prosecuting violations to some regular paid expert or experts, it leaves the whole matter to a board of pharmacy, which receives no compensation from the state and which is virtually responsible only to itself. As to the food and drink act, it leaves the states attorney of each county to prosecute violators on complaint, and, as their time is given to other matters exclusively, complaints, if ever sent in, receive very slight attention at their hands. In view of the widespread prevalence of adulteration, the acts have so far, since their passage in 1881, remained dead letters upon the statute book. We have failed to note a single prosecution under them. All no doubt due to the defect we have pointed out.

The firm above referred to, however, seem determined to comply with the law's requirements. In the circular, they say rather ironically: "We have never sold adulterated or inferior goods, and under our state law we dare not, neither can we compete with those who do. We do not propose to take any precipitate action or involve any of our jobbing friends in trouble. We propose to wait patiently and give them plenty of time to replace their present stocks with pure goods. We do not ask you to buy from us, nor do we contemplate increasing our business in this direction, but we will naturally compel our competitors to ask more for goods, thereby enabling us to realize equal prices for our own.''

The prospect of the passage of a law covering all adulterations by the general government is more remote than immediate. Every state should therefore look to the interests of its own people, and adopt needed measures to check the present general tendency to commercial deceptions. The law should be sweeping in its scope and penalties. It should take in all classes of articles, like the law of Illinois. It should see that rigorous prosecutions are inflicted upon all violators. It should for repeated offenses, impose burdensome penalties and thus force all to abandon their nefarious practices. To effect all this, it should create a board of chemists, under the pay and control of the state, to analyze sample goods from various parts of the state, and then where they find adulterations, leave the courts to pass judgment. With such a provision, the acts of Illinois would be all that could be desired, and offendors would find it exceedingly uncomfortable and unprofitable to ply their business.

Whether viewed from a legal, moral or commercial standpoint, there can be no question as to the baseness of the practice of imposing upon the public. Dr. Hassall has well expressed it when he says: ''It is impossible for a man to be guilty of adulteration and yet be an honest man. Can it even be said of the adulterator, be he a manufacturer or a roaster and grinder of chiccory and coffee, or be he a retail tradesman, who sophisticates the goods which he sells and mixes them with roasted corn or beans, Venetian red, etc., that he is guilty of a less offense than the common thief? The last takes but our property, while the former not only robs us of our substance, but sometimes our health as well.'' ** ''Taking into consideration, therefore, all the circumstances of the case, we believe it to be almost impossible to over-estimate the importance of the subject of adulteration, viewed either as a question of public, of pecuniary loss to the consumer and the revenue or as one of morality. To sum up, it is not too much to say that the question of adulteration is one which affects the health of thousands, and even the lives of many; that hundreds of thousands of pounds (£'s) are annually lost to the consumer by the practice of adulteration; and that by its prevalence the moral status of the commercial portion of the community is lowered in the eyes of the world."

From what has already been shown in this work, it will be apparent that the United States has outstripped all other countries in the extent and variety of the adulterations it has countenanced by a lack of legal restrictions. England in her palmy days, when her merchants were unrestricted, never approached the present practices of some of the merchants of our country. So strongly are the manipulators of our foods banded together that they resist with what influence they can command in a state all efforts to destroy their pernicious business. They are up in protest the moment any one suggests a law. As the New York American Machinist, speaking in a recent issue about commercial dishonesty has well expressed it: "As soon as a measure of this kind is introduced an outcry is sure to be raised against interfering with the rights of trade, as if systematic deception were a vested right which legislatures were bound to protect. While there is nothing on its face derogatory to commercial honesty in making and selling glucose, oleomargarine, clarified syrup, and newly set-up machinery and boilers composed in part of old and worn machines and boilers, there is neither honesty nor should there be cover of law for selling glucose for common "store sugar," oleomargarine for butter, sugar syrup for honey, or reconstructed machinery and boilers for new. Deliberately planned deception should be treated with something more than public contempt, which is no punishment for the kind of individuals who are capable of regularly practicing commercial humbuggery. If there is no law to prevent such deception there ought to be such a force of public indignation brought to bear upon the perpetrators of these tricks, that would effectually drive them either out of business or into strictly honest commercial transactions."

Their chief argument is that in presenting their mixed

substances they keep down the prices of the genuine and thereby benefit poor people. Those who turn out butterine or oleomargarine assert that had there been no such articles in the market, during the winter of 1881 and 1882, the price of butter would have been as high as seventy-five cents per pound, and those who turn out other mixtures defend their practices on the ground that without them many households would be deprived of many indispensible articles. This sort of defense is all very fine so far as it goes, but it wholly ignores the deception at the bottom of their transactions. They claim that their business is all open and above board, but it is a curious commentary upon their statements that whenever there is any likelihood of legislation to compel them to brand their packages so as to indicate their true nature, they at once seek by ambidextrous methods to defeat it. If frauds have been perpetrated, it is always outside speculators and not they who are guilty. If such is the case, then why not let the public be protected against imposition? If they are doing the public a service, why not let the public know exactly what that service is, and not keep them in ignorance of the benefactions bestowed upon them by men, who would have it appear that they are wholly disinterested and have only the welfare (?) of the poor at heart? When people buy their wares, under existing conditions, they suppose they are purchasing the genuine. Why not then allow them to be enlightened as to the true state of affairs and thus enable the poor to rise up and call them blessed and possibly prompt them to erect monuments to their memory on their demise.

The secret of the whole matter is that, if they supinely allowed the passage of a law to compel them to tell the truth, a falling market, small sales, and comparatively small profits would tend to break up their business. The mass of well-to-do people would let their spurious articles alone and poor people would purchase only in case of necessity. At any rate there would be a great falling off in their sales, in their business and in their dividends.

In short, deception is the basis of their success and poor goods their stock in trade, and the sooner they are forced to honest methods, the better for the health and purses of the people and for the integrity of the commercial world.

CONCLUDING OBSERVATIONS.

ON THE USE OF THE MICROSCOPE.

The microscope is used by chemists and the various professions to detect adulterations. It is finely suited for the detection of all organized structures and substances, animal or vegetable, while chemistry is adapted for discovering the presence of various chemical substances and salts. Of course to use it intelligently, one must understand the general character and structure of the substances to be examined, and then any of them are easily designated.

For instance, suppose we have a sample of powdered coffee and chiccory. If we are familiar with their structures, we can at once classify them while inspected under the microscope. However, a knowledge of the organizations of all substances is not necessary. If we have under the microscope a sample bought as coffee at the store and we find that some particles differ from others in general structure, it can be set down as absolutely correct that adulteration with either chiccory or some other article has been resorted to. No matter to how fine a powder the particles may have been reduced, detection is simple and easy. In the case of tea leaves, the genuine leaf will preserve the general outlines—no matter how small the particles—of its structure or cellular tissues, and the presence of foreign leaves can be easily noted. So also the general structure and appearance of wheat flour, sago powder, potato starch, rice, mustard, etc., will reveal their respective differences and enable the observer to note them easily. Likewise in the case of sugar and glucose, the former presents perfect and brilliant crystals while the latter is crystalline in character under examination.

A little practice with different articles will soon make one an expert. A serviceable microscope can be purchased at from $1 and upwards. Every family should possess one and thereby be enabled to examine not only the ingredients of what they consume, liquids as well as solids, but many other articles of use.

INDEX.

www.ingramcontent.com/pod-product-compliance
Lightning Source LLC
Chambersburg PA
CBHW021523270326
41930CB00008B/1059